Religious Studies (AS Philosophy)

Revision Guide Edexcel (Unit 1)

Brian Poxon & Laura Mears

Published by Inducit Learning Ltd trading as pushmepress.com

Mid Somerset House, Southover, Wells

Somerset BA5 1UH, United Kingdom

www.pushmepress.com

First published in 2014

ISBN: 978-1-909618-56-5

Contents

How to Get an A Grade

Effective learning involves reducing difficult topics into smaller, "bite-sized" chunks.

Every revision guide, card or coursebook from PushMe Press comes with its own website consisting of summaries, handouts, games, model essays, revision notes and more. Each website community is supported by the best teachers in the country.

At the end of each chapter you will see an `i-pu-sh` web link that you can type into your web browser along with a QR code that can be scanned by our free app.

These links will give you immediate access to the additional resources you need to "Get an A Grade" by providing you with the relevant information needed.

Getting an A Grade has never been easier.

Download our FREE How to Get an A Grade in Philosophy App for your phone or tablet and get up-to-date information that accompanies this book and the whole PushMe Press range.

http://philosophy.pushmepress.com/download

'The unexamined life is not worth living' Socrates

The Exam

The Edexcel examination for Unit 1 will test your ability to consider and analyse the key concepts; major issues and questions; the contribution of significant people, traditions or movements; religious language and terminology; and the relationship between the areas of study and other aspects of human experience.

You will be asked to answer three questions, in at least two sections, so you have 35 minutes per question (including reading, planning and checking). You can therefore only answer a maximum of two questions from the Philosophy of Religion section: **EITHER** the cosmological argument **OR** the argument from design, and **EITHER** the problem of evil and suffering **OR** miracles.

Most teachers will advise you to revise all four topics thoroughly, as you do not know what form the question will take. Furthermore, many philosophical concepts, scholars and especially vocabulary overlap, so having a well-worn understanding of the key areas will translate into confident, competent writing in the specific area you have chosen to cover.

This said, it is natural that you will have a preference, and every effort should be made to practise every different angle the question may take, completing many timed essays in the lead-up to the examination. At whatever stage you are at in the revision process, whether revising for mocks, or reading this the day before the examination, put your best foot forward; don't focus on what you haven't done, rather make whatever time you have left count.

Introduction to Philosophy of Religion

PHILOSOPHY

Philosophy is "the study of the fundamental nature of knowledge, reality and existence; a set or system of beliefs". (Oxford Dictionary)

This can be a painful, frustrating, but hopefully enlightening process of dismantling what you had previously considered sure, and re-building on new or improved foundations.

In the case of religion, philosophy is the critical study and analysis of certain elements and concepts of religions. In a Western context, this means the Judaeo-Christian tradition, so we are usually considering whether God exists, and if so, what his character is like. Although in some contexts, it will be possible and appropriate to speak of "gods", and consider approaches in Eastern religions (for example, in the Religious Experience section of the A2 course), or even ancient civilisations, we will usually use the singular, definitive, "God".

The first part of our study, therefore, is about whether there are any convincing arguments about the existence of God:

- Is there **DESIGN** in the universe that points to a designer (the teleological argument)?

- Do the origins, nature and order of the cosmos point to an external supreme intellect (the **COSMOLOGICAL ARGUMENT**)?

The second part of our study considers selected problems in the Philosophy of Religion:

- Does the existence of evil and suffering rule out the existence of an all-powerful, benevolent being (the problem of evil)?

- Do miracles happen, and if so, do they point to the existence of an all-powerful, benevolent being (miracles)?

We now turn to part 1 - the arguments, where we consider what form a good basis for knowledge would take.

EMPIRICISM

EMPIRICISM holds that the most reliable forms of knowledge are gained through experience, especially of the senses. Arguments that begin from observations of the world are **A POSTERIORI**; based on, or after (post), empirical evidence. They use **INDUCTIVE** reasoning, which means that knowledge is inferred from observation of specific instances. Such knowledge will usually be expressed in terms of **SYNTHETIC STATEMENTS** - where the predicate is not contained within the subject, for example "married men are happy", where happiness isn't necessarily part of being married, and some knowledge of the world is required to assess its validity.

The empirical arguments we study at AS (Edexcel) are: the argument from design (the teleological argument) and the cosmological argument. They are a posteriori because they start from looking at the world's features and processes, and conclude (eventually) from these observations, that God exists.

RATIONALISM

RATIONALISM is a theory of knowledge which holds that the most reliable forms of knowledge are gained independently of sensory experience. An **A PRIORI** argument is something true by definition, from reason and before (prior to) empirical evidence. It uses **DEDUCTIVE** reasoning, which means that the conclusion necessarily follows from the premises. Such reasoning will always be expressed in terms of an **ANALYTIC STATEMENT** - a statement where the predicate is contained within the subject, for example, "married men are husbands".

The AS level syllabus does not include a rationalist argument for the existence of God, yet it is helpful to be aware of how a rationalist might criticise an empirical argument, and vice versa, so you can explain why an empirical argument might be considered weak or strong.

The Cosmological Argument for the Existence of God

KEY TERMS

- **A POSTERIORI** - Knowledge gained after experience.
- **CONTINGENT EXISTENCE** - Something which, by its nature, does not necessarily have to exist, and could or could not have existence, eg you or me. Once existent, can go out of existence.
- **COSMOLOGICAL ARGUMENT** - Reasoning concerning the origins, nature and order of the cosmos.
- **FALLACY** - An error in reasoning that renders an argument invalid or unsound, even when looking like it is logically plausible.
- **INDUCTION** - A type of reasoning that takes specific instances and from them, draws a general conclusion (eg as seen in the cosmological argument).
- **INFINITE REGRESS** - In the cosmological argument, this refers to a chain of causes going back that has no beginning.
- **NECESSARY BEING** - A being whose non-existence is a contradiction.
- **PHENOMENAL** - Things which are perceived by the senses or by immediate experience.

AQUINAS' COSMOLOGICAL ARGUMENT

The cosmological argument stands in contrast to the OA in that it is not deductive but **INDUCTIVE**. Aquinas put forward five ways for the existence of God, and the cosmological argument (CA) was outlined in the first three of those ways; Aquinas argued for the existence of God from **MOTION, CAUSE** and **NECESSITY**.

Aquinas commenced his argument with the **A POSTERIORI** evidence of the universe itself and asked why it existed (not just why there are things within the universe, but why there is a universe at all). Upon analysing such evidence, Aquinas noted that some things are in motion. By motion, Aquinas meant the change that goes on in particular things within the universe, such as within a tree as it grows taller or sheds bark. (Note here that for Aquinas, following Aristotle, motion did not just mean physical movement, as something could be still and yet be changing, like the aforementioned tree).

For something to be in motion it must be, in Aquinas' words, **MOVED BY ANOTHER** (something external to it). He gave an example of wood, which is changed/acted upon by fire to reach its potential of becoming hot. The change, Aquinas noted, could not be caused by the thing itself; something acted/moved to make the wood hot (fire), but then something moved to make the fire (friction), and so on.

Aquinas considered the possibility of this chain of motion going backwards infinitely (infinite regress) to get to an ultimate explanation for motion, but noted that this was not possible.

> *"There would then be no first mover, and, consequently, no subsequent mover, as subsequent movers move only insofar as they are moved by the first mover."* Aquinas

Aquinas, working from Aristotle, understood this first or prime, unmoved mover to be God.

Aquinas' second way is his argument from **FIRST CAUSE**. Nothing is its own efficient cause as it would "have to exist prior to itself", which is impossible. Again, it is not possible to go back infinitely in the chain of causes as without a first cause there would be no subsequent intermediate causes which would mean that there would be no present effects (things we see in place around us now). "Plainly this is not the case", noted Aquinas, "so we must admit a first efficient cause (itself uncaused) which everyone calls 'God'."

Aquinas' third way is based upon the idea of **NECESSITY** and **CONTINGENCY**. Contingent things are those things which could or could not be in existence, they are non-permanent; if they come into being, they go out of being. Because of that, "it is impossible for them always to exist, for that which is possible not to be at some time does not exist. If everything is like that, at one time nothing existed.* If that were true, there would be nothing in existence now, because things only come to exist because of things already existing."

Thus Aquinas posits the need for a necessary being whose necessity lies in itself because if everything was only contingent then there would be nothing today.

If there was a state of nothingness, which Aquinas argues would have been the case without one necessary thing, then **EX NIHILO NIHIL FIT**, (out of nothing, nothing comes), and yet there is something - so there must be something that has necessary existence. Things do not have to exist, but they do, and this could not be the case if everything was entirely contingent. The required necessary being is God, unmoved mover and first cause.

*As there is nothing necessary about their existence, given infinite time there would be a stage where nothing existed. Jackson very neatly suggests that if we added up the life-span of every contingent thing, we would never reach infinity, so there must be a time when nothing existed, if everything is contingent.

COPLESTON'S COSMOLOGICAL ARGUMENT AND RUSSELL'S RESPONSE

In 1948, a famous debate between **COPLESTON** and **RUSSELL** outlined key differences in understandings of any ultimate explanation for the universe. Copleston's argument from **CONTINGENCY** relied on the argument from Liebniz' **PRINCIPLE OF SUFFICIENT REASON**. Liebniz asked why there is something rather than nothing, which led him to look for an ultimate reason for the existence of the universe. He argued that there needs to be "sufficient reason" to explain why something is the case. With regard to the existence of the universe, this sufficient reason cannot be given from the collection or sum of its constituent parts, as these are insufficient to explain the whole thing. The sufficient reason must be external to the universe because contingent things don't explain their own existence but are reliant on other contingent things.

This principle, and the way in which it is disputed, is central to the debate between Copleston and Russell. In summary, the argument went along the following lines:

- Copleston put forward the need for a **PRINCIPLE OF SUFFICIENT REASON** that is not found within the collection of contingent beings within the universe.

- Russell asked for clarification of such a principle, and wanted to know when precisely a sufficient reason is reached, and if sufficient reason for existence is the same as **CAUSE**.

Copleston noted that we can attribute cause to things that are contingent but that sufficient reason refers to a total explanation as to how the universe as a whole is in existence, not just those contingent things within it, which rely on being caused.

He stressed the inability of contingent things to provide their own sufficient reason; the reason for their existence must lie outside of them. If God is another contingent being, then he cannot have within him the complete reason for his own existence.

As a necessary (not contingent) being, God is his own sufficient cause.

Russell questioned the need for a sufficient reason, and whether such was possible anyway. He questioned if it is possible to go from contingent causes within the universe to a necessary sufficient and external reason, and wondered how such a move would be possible. Russell also said that necessary only applied to **ANALYTIC** statements such as "a bachelor is an unmarried man", and saw no ground to talk of God as necessary.

Copleston responded by saying that just because a thing has not been found (the sufficient reason) it is not the same as saying it should not be looked for.

The contingent cause of events cannot provide a sufficient reason for the whole series; hence the need for a necessary being. Copleston also suggested that Russell's unwillingness to enter the debate concerning a principle of sufficient reason is dogmatic; if a person refuses to come to the chessboard then a game cannot commence.

Russell maintained that the world "just is"; it is **BRUTE FACT**. And that it is not possible to go from causes within the universe to a cause of the universe (famously saying that just because every human being has a mother, it does not mean the entire race has a mother). Here he is accusing Copleston of the **FALLACY OF COMPOSITION**, which assumes that what is true of parts must be true of the whole.

Copleston replied that God as a necessary being is not a first cause or mother as such, as that would mean God is another "phenomenal" and contingent cause, which would not explain the whole series. God is an **ONTOLOGICAL NECESSITY**. Copleston went on to suggest that Russell was denying the reality of the problem regarding the existence of the universe by arguing it "just is". Who is right, Copleston or Russell here?

HUME'S CRITICISMS OF THE COSMOLOGICAL ARGUMENT:

Hume questioned why the world needs a first cause or a beginning. Why is infinite regress impossible? Even if we see cause and effect in the world (and Hume questioned this assumption), it does not mean that the universe itself be the effect of an uncaused cause, but the chain of causes could simply continue ad infinitum.

Furthermore, Hume famously challenged our understanding of cause and effect, noting that event a following event b does not meant that a caused b, even if we have not seen one instance when b did not happen after a. His argument noted that we put cause and effect together by habit rather than having any evidence that one caused the other. Hume's argument continues to carry much weight today and his questioning of cause has implications for Aquinas' claim that God is the first cause.

Hume questioned why there could not be more than one cause. The empirical evidence from the world gives no clues as to the number of causes that it required (if it required any), and, without being able to go outside the universe, Hume questioned how we would know if there was one or more causes. Maybe male and female Gods who are born and then die are more fitting from the empirical evidence we see in the world **IF EFFECTS RESEMBLE CAUSES** in any way - such Gods may fit the profile of the a posteriori evidence more closely than a Christian God. To stress, Hume, writing as an empiricist (and, remember, Aquinas is working from an a posteriori base), noted that we have no experience of the causer(s) of the universe, which seems to be a unique case; we have experience of what we have called cause and effect within the world but how can we know about a cause outside the world; on what experience would we base such?

Hume questioned if the uniting of different things within the universe together and saying that "the whole" has a cause is **AN ARBITRARY ACT OF THE MIND**. There is nothing in our experience, or any logical argument that can be made, to suggest that there is an overarching cause which gives a reason for the effects we see in the universe.

In response, Elizabeth **ANSCOMBE** has questioned Hume's argument about not being able to say that existence has not got a cause because we cannot go outside the universe to know that. She writes that it is possible to conclude that "existence must have a cause" without knowing specifically "that particular effects must have particular causes". Whilst it is possible to imagine things coming into existence without a cause, this does not tell us if this is the case in reality.

STRENGTHS

- Could Aquinas' argument from causation actually tie together with scientific evidence of causation? Some scientists argue that Big Bang cosmology requires a causal factor. With the discovery of the Higgs Boson particle, the question still remains why such an important particle is in place. If we accept that we need to find an ultimate explanation or, as Leibniz stressed, a sufficient reason, do the arguments of Aquinas and Copleston still offer some useful ground?

- Is the discovery of effects without causes sufficient to fatally attack Aquinas' causation argument? Could it be that the cause of such effects has not yet been discovered rather than there not being a cause for them?

- The progress of science would cease if we took Russell's line "things just are". The developments we have seen are because we have attempted to answer the question, "why are things the way they are; what is the explanation in this and that case?" Perhaps Copleston was actually being more scientific in his quest for an answer to the whole series of events.

WEAKNESSES

- In the field of Quantum Mechanics, research is being carried out as to the idea of "backward causation", and even the notion of uncaused events, and it is possible that our whole notion of what is meant by cause and effect will need to be re-evaluated. It may also be possible that matter or energy is eternal, and as such the necessary element of Aquinas' argument is not God but material itself. We can still ask, however, why that it is the case that matter has an eternal nature ("it just has" might be Russell's response, and this is an acceptable position for many).

- Does a cause that once existed have to exist today? Imagine someone who throws a model glider off the top of a cliff; the glider on its journey continues to move despite the person who threw it not being any longer involved in its ongoing motion and journey through the air. Does this mean the argument for God being the first cause has no relevance or importance anymore because his job has been completed, just as the thrower of the glider has completed her work? This argument does not understand what Aquinas was actually saying, as he was asking why there is **ANY MOVEMENT AT ALL**, rather than just proposing God as some kind of first pusher of a chain of events. For Aquinas, God is not the one who winds up the clockwork mouse and leaves it to run, but rather the one who is the necessary mover, the cause of all causes whose activity, unlike the one who winds up the mouse, has not ceased. God, for Aquinas, is the ultimate explanation for why there is cause or movement, the ultimate cause, without whom there is no ongoing universe, cause, movement or any contingent things.

- It is perhaps not difficult to understand that a string of contingent beings could always be in existence, overlapping in the time that they have being. This would mean, contrary to Aquinas' argument, that there never was a time when nothing existed, even from a contingent basis. Alternatively, could there be things which have always been in existence but will go out of existence at some time in the future?

- Does the universe need a "sufficient reason", or is it, as Russell said, "brute fact"? Is there a need for a cause outside of the world to explain its existence? Is there an overarching sufficient reason for existence? If so, why? But, is Russell's reply of "brute fact", "the universe just is", a very unphilosophical (almost anti-philosophical) approach which should not be encouraged in students?

- Does Copleston's cosmological argument suffer from the same difficulties that the ontological argument does when needing a Necessary Being for it to work? Whilst the concept of a necessary being might be possible, that does not make such a reality.

KEY QUOTES

1. *"The First-Cause argument rests on the assumption that every series must have a first term, which is false; for example, the series of proper fractions has no first term."* Russell

2. *"To say that such a very complex and well-ordered universe comes into being without any cause or reason is equivalent to throwing one's hands up in the air and just saying that anything at all might happen."* Keith Ward

3. *"The series has not a phenomenal cause but a transcendent cause,' to which Russell responds, 'that's always assuming that not only every particular thing in the world, but the world as a whole must have a cause. For that assumption I see no ground whatever."* Copleston replies:

4. *"Though difficult, and still incomplete, there is no reason to believe that the greatest problem, how the universe came into being, and what it is, will not be solved; we can safely presume that the solution will be comprehensible to human minds."* Atkins

5. *"Not how the world is, but that it is, is the mystery."* Wittgenstein

CONFUSIONS TO AVOID

The easy reply to Aquinas which is often given, which runs along the lines of "if everything needs a cause, what caused God?" is perhaps not the strongest one to make, in that it does not understand what Aquinas regards as cause or what he is suggesting we should understand God to be. God is not "one other thing" or the first flicker of the line of dominoes, but the necessary unmoved cause on whom all other movement, change, cause and contingency is reliant.

Be very careful to understand and able to explain the **DIFFERENCES** between the cosmological arguments of Aquinas and Copleston; they are related, but different and the use of Liebniz' Principle of Sufficient Reason will help you in your delineation of these differences.

Likewise, beware of over-emphasising the Kalaam version over that of Aquinas. Although both stem from Aristotle, the Kalaam version simply argues for a first cause or **CREATOR**, whereas Aquinas argues for both a **CREATOR** and **SUSTAINER**. Think of this circus skill; with one big whirl, the entertainer sets the plate spinning on his stick, but as it starts to wobble, he flicks his wrist to keep the plate in motion. Consider the world around; is it moving steadily as if sustained, or is it wobbling as if set in motion, then abandoned? How we interpret our experience may help us to favour one version over the other, and evaluating different versions of the argument is a good skill to hone. However, it may be interesting to consider whether the Kalaam version is an argument for God's existence at all: the God of Islam (Allah) is a God who sees, and interacts with his creation, administering justice through reward and punishment, not a god who set the world in motion, then retreated.

KANT puts forward a rather different sort of criticism of the argument (which also applies to the argument from design). In contrast to the materialists, who accept the empirical starting point, Kant flatly rejects any attempt to argue God into existence - be it empirical or rational. We should "deny knowledge, in order to make room for faith" (from Critique of Pure Reason). Yet it should not be concluded from this that Kant is an atheist. For Kant, God is a **TRANSCENDENT** being, who is above and beyond our sensory experience and powers of reason. His existence is, therefore, neither proved nor disproved by argument. "You cannot move from physical premises to a metaphysical conclusion. We can, in other words, know about the **PHENOMENA** but not the **NOUMENA**." (Peter Vardy)

GET MORE HELP

Get more help with the cosmological argument by using the links below:

http://i-pu.sh/B7N62J29

The Teleological (Design) Argument for the Existence of God

KEY TERMS

- **ANALOGY** - Where two things are compared as similar because they share common features (for example, a watchmaker designing and giving purpose to a watch and a world-maker designing and giving purpose to a world).

- **A POSTERIORI** - Knowledge gained after experience; in this case, arguing from the experience of design and regularity in the universe to God.

- **DESIGN QUA PURPOSE** - Design as it relates to purpose, in this case the purpose for which things seem to be designed.

- **DESIGN QUA REGULARITY** - Design as it relates to regularity, in this case the regularity in the universe and how it works.

- **EMPIRICISM** - A position which holds that knowledge only comes through sensory experience.

- **SCEPTIC** - A person who seeks to rigorously question, challenge and assess the evidence put forward within arguments which make knowledge claims.

- **TELEOLOGICAL** - Telos refers to end or purpose, and whether, in this instance, there is an end purpose for which the universe is designed.

- **THEORY OF EVOLUTION THROUGH NATURAL SELECTION** - The theory accredited to Darwin which accounts for the survival of species through natural selection not design.

Like the **COSMOLOGICAL ARGUMENT**, the teleological argument for the existence of God is an **A POSTERIORI** argument which attempts to show that the design, order, regularity and purpose of the universe imply the existence of a God who gives such characteristics to it. It is important to remember that the two teleological arguments studied were written before the theory of evolution through natural selection was articulated.

AQUINAS' TELEOLOGICAL ARGUMENT

AQUINAS put forward a form of the **TA** in the fifth of his five ways referred to earlier. This argument is often known as **DESIGN QUA REGULARITY**, (though you will also see it referred to as design qua purpose) which means design "as relating to/pertaining to" regularity. The regularity refers to the order and pattern of things in the universe, such as the blossom that appears on trees regularly in the spring as if it was working to a pattern or order (many other examples from nature can be given).

In observing the world, Aquinas stated that objects which have no intelligence of their own function in an efficient way and achieve the best possible results.

This seems to be because they have been designed or directed to do so. He goes on to note, as a result of this observation:

"Things that lack knowledge cannot move purposely unless they are directed by some intelligent being: an arrow needs an archer

to shoot it. Therefore there must exist some intelligent being who directs all things to the PURPOSE for which they exist. This being we call God."

Just as the archer directs the arrow, Aquinas stated that God has given a direction to natural bodies, which have no rational powers to direct themselves, to enable them to reach their goal. There is an order and **REGULARITY** in nature seen in physical laws through which things reach their telos or end. This regularity and order is not produced by the objects themselves, or by chance, but has been given by an intelligent being, God.

PALEY'S TELEOLOGICAL ARGUMENT

PALEY'S argument utilised design qua purpose as well as design qua regularity, and he made use of an analogy to draw conclusions about the nature of the world and the need for a designer who provides purpose and regularity. In this first part of his argument he was referring particularly to **DESIGN QUA PURPOSE**.

Paley asks the reader to imagine the scenario where someone bumps their foot on a stone as they are walking across a heath; on doing so, the person might not be drawn to ask where the stone came from as there is nothing particularly noticeable or special about it.

However, if the person was then to stumble across a pocket watch, (at the time a recent and impressive invention), they would immediately see that this object was more complex; within its mechanism a whole series of cogs and springs are seen to work together towards the aim of enabling the watch to tell the time. The observer might notice that it is due to the precise way in which the watch pieces were placed that the purpose of the watch is fulfilled, and there is a skill involved in placing these pieces together in exactly that order (and no other). From this, Paley notes that it is required that a **WATCHMAKER/DESIGNER** had put the complex mechanism together for its **SPECIFIC PURPOSE**.

From this basic premise of design, Paley moves on to the observation of the natural world, where much more complex elements such as the human eye work precisely together towards the purpose of seeing; the parts of the eye such as the cornea and the lens have to be put together in exactly the right manner to fulfil the purpose of seeing which suggests that a skilled designer, as in the case of the watch, is once again needed.

The intricacy and **CAREFUL ORDERING** of the design is far too precise for it to have come about that way by chance, and it does its job efficiently only because of that specific design which enables it to fulfil its purpose. Paley was fascinated by the natural world and used many other examples from nature, such as the precise number of teats on different animals which are suitable for the litter they have, to draw the conclusion that the giver of design qua purpose in the natural world is God.

Working against the backdrop of **NEWTONIAN PHYSICS** and the formulation of the laws of motion, Paley then went on to note how the universe also has an **ORDER** and **REGULARITY** to its movements, where it works according to predictable patterns which could not be generated by non-conscious objects. The precise order of planetary movement and the essential operation of gravity within specific natural laws, which lie within very narrow limits, impressed upon Paley how regularity is essential for life to take place on Earth.

In a similar way to Aquinas, Paley drew the conclusion that such regularity and order is given by an external agent, God.

Paley is thus working from design, **A POSTERIORI** from effect to cause, using analogy to work with the idea that just as man-made objects, made for a purpose, require an intelligent designer, so the design in the universe requires an intelligent designer; purpose and regularity in nature point to one who provides such.

Paley noted that his argument was not weakened if one had not seen a watch before; one would still infer a watch designer, and different conclusions would be drawn with regard to the source of the watch than that of the rock. Further, one did not need to understand how the watch was made, or how the parts work together. Paley even made note that at times the watch goes wrong, but that this did not invalidate the idea of it being designed. He also rejected the idea that it was the human mind that placed the idea of design upon the watch. These additional notes were implicitly addressing **HUME'S** criticisms of the argument from design.

CHALLENGES TO THE TELEOLOGICAL ARGUMENT FROM HUME, MILL AND DARWINISM

Hume

Whilst **HUME** pre-dated **PALEY**, he argued that the TA failed on several points. Hume was an **EMPIRICIST** and a **SCEPTIC**; an empiricist looks for observable evidence gained through sensory experience from which to attain any knowledge about the world, whilst a sceptic challenges arguments, and studies proposed evidence carefully before making judgement, realising the limitations of knowledge and the difficulty of reaching certainty. It is important that you bear this in mind as you go through Hume's challenges to the teleological argument.

Hume questioned the validity of Paley's **WATCH ANALOGY**. A watch works using strict mechanical movements, and Paley extrapolated from this that the world has similar hallmarks of design. Hume argued that this is not actually how the world "looks"; it appears more organic in nature; it grows and develops on its own. Such things as cabbages and carrots are natural things, whereas the watch is not, which is why we pick it up and look at it carefully. Wilkinson and Campbell note that, "by choosing a machine as our analogy, we have already determined the outcome we want". For this reason, to go from arguing that a watch needs a watchmaker and compare this to a world which needs a world maker is to use a flawed analogy.

The fact that evil exists in the world runs counter to Paley's claim that the designer is the God of **CLASSICAL THEISM** who is both all-good and all-powerful. Would such a God have created a world that exhibits evil? If God did design the world and leave it to run not only does the design he put in the world seem faulty and amoral but it hardly speaks of a personal and good God who is still interested in it. (Remember, Aquinas and Paley were not suggesting God was a disinterested Aristotelian Prime Mover.)

Indeed, from the a posteriori evidence that Paley wants to use, it is very unclear that this would lead to posit an **INFINITE** God as creator, (as the world is finite), or a **PERFECT** God, (as the world is not perfect).

Hume suggested that such a world, if effects resemble causes, speaks more of an infant or inferior deity as its creator, a creator who was "ashamed of his lame performance".

Such a designer might also no longer be alive.

Hume asks how it is possible to arrive at the idea of **ONE DESIGNER** of the universe from the evidence we have. Even the watch might involve several designers, such as the designers of the springs and the cogs. If apparently straightforward things within the world require a team of designers, is it not just as feasible, if Paley wants to retain the use of his analogy, that a team of designers, each with different skills, were required to design the universe? Paley might respond that God has all skills, but then this is a faith statement rather than an outcome directly derived from his watchmaker analogy.

Hume noted that we have **EXPERIENCE** of seeing how machines or houses are made, but do not have this for the designing of a universe. Therefore, how can we possibly know that this world was designed without being able to step outside the world to see such a process, as we can do when we observe the designing of a house? Using such experience we legitimately note that such design was due to an architect. And even seeing order in the universe does not suggest an order giver; how, indeed, would we know this world is ordered if we have no other world with which to compare it?

If the **INTRICATE COMPLEXITY** of the world requires an intelligent designer, then why doesn't an intelligent mind require a designer, and so on, and so on? Hume wondered why we would stop at God when seeking an explanation for intelligent design.

Although pre-dating Darwin, Hume argued that there could be many other ways to explain apparent design, including the idea that in an infinite universe this particular world could be the one where a stable combination of atoms (Hume would not have used that word) enabled this world to arise. Hume is here working with an understanding of the universe known as the **EPICUREAN HYPOTHESIS**, in which it was argued that natural forces gradually form into order from chaos. An analogy is that, given enough time, monkeys left with a typewriter would type out a Shakespearean sonnet; this would not, however, be through intelligent aforethought, but randomly as one of many possibilities which, given time, would happen. Where stability is evident, **PALEY** has read design, order and purpose given by a designer, but Hume argued that such a leap is not implied at all as there are other explanations for such order; simply put, if it were chaotic then the world would not have survived.

Responses to Hume

Is he correct to say, when questioning Paley's analogy, that different things, such as watches and worlds, cannot be compared? It is common practice to extract similarities between very different types of objects (for example, principles of flight in an insect and a helicopter). Does Paley's comparison of design in both the watch and the world thus stand?

Swinburne has criticised Hume for suggesting the possibility of a multitude of creators as going against **OCKHAM'S RAZOR**, where the explanation with the fewer unnecessary complications is to be preferred when arguments are being compared.

Flew has questioned the "monkeys typing out a Shakespearean sonnet" analogy as completely unfounded and not a comparison that can be used with the multitudinous factors that have to come together in a precise fashion for this world to form. He argues that following where the evidence leads from the complexity of the universe suggests an intelligent designer as the more probable and plausible explanation (rather than a proof).

Mill

The natural world is unbearably cruel and violent and animals do things which if they were human they would be tried for; things such as certain animals giving their prey a lingering and agonising death hardly give evidence of a creator who is wise and all-loving when creating and designing. **NATURE** itself, through its inbuilt processes like earthquakes and hurricanes, causes untold misery and destruction. This argument is formed after the publication of **DARWIN'S** On the Origin of Species and takes note of the harsh, remorseless and unsympathetic way in which species die out if they do not adapt to the environment.

As Mill, like Hume, was an **EMPIRICIST**, he evaluated the evidence of the world before him and noted that, if there was a creator, then he certainly was not the God suggested by classical theism. It could not be deduced from a world that contains barbaric evil that God was all-knowing, all-loving and all-powerful, just or, indeed, worthy of worship. Such a maker seems to not just allow but will suffering. In support of Mill, **DAWKINS** argues that God must be a sadist who enjoys spectator sports if the same God made the tiger and the lamb, the cheetah and the gazelle.

Responses to Mill

Is nature "cruel" or just natural? Is "cruel" a human interpretation of events that are simply part of survival? Does an earthquake have "thought" about its effects, and are these natural processes actually both necessary and "good" for enabling human life to survive (if human life is seen as a "good" thing)? **MILL** might respond by saying that it really takes a particularly distorted view to call such atrocities in nature good.

Darwin

The theory of evolution through natural selection states that those species whose **MUTATIONS** fail to suit their environment die out, and the genes of those who were able to survive are passed on (be careful though, as Darwin did not know that genes were passed on or of **DNA**). It is therefore not design that enables a certain species to survive, but evolution which operates "blind", working along the lines of "survival of the fittest".

Dawkins argues that it is DNA that controls the destiny of a species, including human beings, and not the other way round, and this applies to every life form on Earth.

Apparent design, such as strong beaks on birds, are actually just features of those birds who have had mutations within their genes and benefited from the stronger beaks which enables them to get the food that birds with weaker beaks could not crack open. Those with such strong beaks then survive and reproduce, passing on the strong beak genes. Those birds whose genes undergo other random mutations, ones that do not help the bird survive, mean that such birds just die out, and so we are left with what might look like design as birds have the beaks they need. But birds without those beaks would simply no longer be in existence. This argument does follow the principle of Ockham's Razor as it does not imply any external agent of whom we have no evidence.

Beneficial changes aid efficiency and therefore secure survival. Whilst the operation of certain species looks quite complex due to many minute natural changes and countless adaptations over time, this is not to be confused with **DESIGN FOR PURPOSE** given by an external agent. There is no overriding purposeful design to elements within the universe, or any overriding pattern or regulated plan that joins the whole thing together; evolution is not heading anywhere. Homo sapiens and other species are those creatures who have had the mutations that have adapted them to this current environment - survival is the only "driver", but this is not governed by any external force or design agent.

Humans are, however, a species that have "progressed" or mutated into exhibiting rationality, which runs counter to the idea of Genesis, that man has fallen from a higher state of grace to a lower state of sin.

Responses to Darwin

Although the process of evolution has been called blind, it is still possible to ask if the process as a whole has some element of design given to it. How is it that the world is so organised that evolution can take place? Has God placed the very precise natural laws within the world which allow evolution to occur? With increased knowledge of the universe as a whole, it has become evident that the conditions which support life have to be very precisely ordered and a single minute factor different to the ones in place would not have resulted in the possibility of life or evolution. **DAWKINS** and **RUSSELL** might respond that this is the world just "as it is", and we only know that this is the world we have because we have evolved to tell the story.

FR TENNANT (1866-1957) was a theologian who accepted the theory of evolution. Yet rather than seeing it as a challenge to belief in a designer God, he considered evolutionary theory to strengthen the case for divine belief. The **ANTHROPIC PRINCIPLE** reflects his observation that the conditions on Earth are set up perfectly for life to develop, and the chances of this happening are so slim, as to warrant belief in a designer God. (Ockham's Razor can apply here - which is simpler; that a God designed the universe's features and laws so as to warrant life, or that it all happened randomly?)

Tennant's second argument is his **AESTHETIC ARGUMENT**, or the argument from beauty. Beauty is "a biologically superfluous accompaniment of the cosmic process", which means that it is not necessary for the continuance of life. Why, then, is it in evidence in the world? The answer, he argues, is that God designed things to be beautiful for his own enjoyment, as well as the delight of his creatures. This argument brings God's benevolence, as well as his omniscience and omnipotence, into play.

STRENGTHS

- We can think of **NATURAL LAWS** that Aquinas would not have known in any scientific detail, such as gravity, and agree that they do work according to a regular pattern so that bricks do not fly upwards when dropped. Is his reading of the regularity in nature correct to the extent that we question things when they seem not to follow a pattern or regularity?

- As our knowledge of the **INTRICACY** of the universe grows, and how millions of factors have to be very precise for the Earth, let alone human life, to exist as it does, would this support Paley's argument that there seems to be design and regularity? Although writing at a time of great scientific advance, during which the world was increasingly viewed mechanistically, neither Hume nor Paley would have had access to today's scientific data regarding the fine-tuned precision of the universe. Would this support Paley's argument?

- Does evolution through natural selection provide sufficient **REASON** to explain the universe as a whole? Does it still require an instigator/designer? Do very precise conditions within the universe, which allow for the process of evolution to take place, simply arise by chance? In any other field where such finely tuned conditions come together we might say that someone has made sure those precise systems have been placed together at certain temperatures and distances; would chance be a poor scientific response in that case? Is science being true to itself by suggesting evolution happens naturally, or is it valid to still look for the reason why evolution takes place?

WEAKNESSES

- **INTERPRETATION OF EXPERIENCE** - As a general point it is worth asking if everything serve a purpose, or the best purpose, on every occasion? Is purpose placed on things by human observers?

- **LIMITATIONS OF ANALOGY** - Whilst a watch implies an external designer, natural things can be produced by natural means. It could be argued that there is design within the natural order, but this does not necessarily mean that such design was given from an external agent in the way the watch received its design.

- How strong are teleological arguments now that the theory of evolution through natural selection has much scientific evidence with which to support the idea that natural adaptation explains apparent signs of design? Hume might say that we have no way of knowing that evolution is the explanation rather than design, but, as an empiricist, **THE PROBABILITY IS GREATER**.

KEY QUOTES

1. *"If Aquinas had lived today, he would doubtless have argued that the evolutionary hypothesis supports rather than invalidates the conclusion of the argument ... [and that it] clearly points to an extrinsic intelligent author of [non-intelligent material], who operates for a purpose."* Copleston

2. *"The way in which living things work, which requires a huge coordination of lots of tiny bits, each doing their specific job, is amazingly complex. This coordination, the detail and intricacy of interrelations between parts, suggests planning - a plan that follows a purpose."* Lacewing.

3. The parts of the watch are *"put together for a purpose, eg, they are so formed and adjusted as to produce motion, and that motion so regulated as to point out the hour of the day ... Every indication of contrivance, every manifestation of design, which existed in the watch, exists in the works of nature [and those] contrivances of nature surpass the contrivance of art, in the complexity, subtlety, and curiosity of the mechanism."* Paley

4. For stars to form, the *"initial strength of the explosion in the Big Bang had to be precise to one part in 10 to the power of 60. That's as precise as hitting a one-inch target at the other side of the observable universe ... Science cannot explain why the Big Bang was exactly the size or why the laws of nature are the way they are ... one obvious explanation is that the Big Bang, the properties of matter-energy, the laws of nature, were all designed to allow life to evolve."* Lacewing

5. *"There is a danger of turning the argument from design on its head. Human arms were not divinely designed to be at the exact level of door-handles - it was the other way round. Hen's eggs are not providentially planned to fit exactly into egg-cups - it is the other way round."* Richards

6. *"In a universe of blind physical forces and genetic replication, some people are going to get hurt, other people are going to get lucky, and you won't find any rhyme or reason in it, nor any justice. The universe we observe has precisely the properties we should expect if there is, at bottom, no design, no purpose, no evil and no good, nothing but blind pitiless indifference."* Dawkins

7. *"Everything, in short, which the worst men commit either against life or property is perpetrated on a larger scale by natural agents."* Mill

8. *"We find it hard to look at anything without wondering what it is 'for', what the motive for it is, or the purpose behind it."* [But we should not read] *"malevolent purpose into what is actually bad luck."* Dawkins

9. *"Many of the questions religion tries to answer are not real questions ... the question concerning the purpose of the universe is, an entirely invented question."* Atkins in Taylor

10. *"The only watchmaker in nature is the blind force of physics."* Dawkins

CONFUSIONS TO AVOID

- Do not suggest Mill was arguing that the world was not designed. Although he might well have thought that it wasn't, the thrust of his argument was that the evidence simply did not suggest that the designer of the world was all-good, all-powerful, all-knowing and just, as the Judeao-Christian tradition, including Aquinas and Paley, believed.
- Darwin's work did not set out to attack the design argument. Whilst Darwin realised that the consequences of his theory were that the world as science was now beginning to understand it did not require a designer, he remained agnostic, and other factors in his life, such as the death of his daughter, had bearing on his own faith position.
- Be wary of using the word "chance" to describe Dawkins' position on how the world came to be. The word "random" is perhaps a more accurate description of how his view differs from that of design.

GET MORE HELP

Get more help with the teleological argument by using the links below:

http://i-pu.sh/H0W32D53

Miracles

KEY TERMS

- **DEISM** - The belief that God has no further involvement in the world after creating it.

- **INDUCTION** - "Instances of which we have had no experience resemble those of which we have had experience", Hume.

- **MIRACLE** - From the Latin "miraculum" - an object of wonder.

- **THEISM** - The belief that God not only creates the world but is actively involved in it through miracles.

Three key definitions of miracle will be explored. Each requires different analyses and evaluation.

DEFINITION 1: BREAKING NATURAL LAW

In An Enquiry Concerning Human Understanding, **HUME** defined a miracle as: **A TRANSGRESSION OF A NATURAL LAW BY A PARTICULAR VIOLATION OF THE DEITY**. It is important to realise here that Hume is not saying that a miracle is simply an extraordinary or unusual event, but one which breaks natural law, and is carried out through the will of the Deity. This was in contrast to **AQUINAS**, who, in one description of miracle, suggested that God could speed up nature, or do things in a different way to nature, neither of which required the breaking of a natural law.

An example of a transgression of a natural law in the Bible is seen in **JOSHUA 10**, where the sun is recorded as standing still in the sky for a full day. The natural law of the rotation of the Earth is broken during that event. Using his definition, Hume argued against viewing such events as miracles. As an empiricist, he argued that knowledge requires evidence, and we have to take a sceptical approach to anything requiring our assent. Bearing this in mind, his argument against miracles was as follows:

1. There is evidence for the idea that the laws of nature are highly likely to hold; these are established through many trials and repetition of experiments, as well as experience, and we make judgements about future likelihood of events based on these previous examples. We have countless examples of the sun rising and therefore it is highly probable that it will rise and not stand still in the sky. This projecting forward to suggest future events will take place based on previous evidence is called the **PRINCIPLE OF INDUCTION**. Hume did accept that what happened countless times in the past did not guarantee such would happen again in the future, even though that would

probably be the case. Because of this problem of induction, it is necessary to look both at the evidence and the testimony of witnesses to assess its likelihood.

2. Once we do this, then Hume says that we must ask the question, is there more evidence for a miracle occurring or for the natural law holding? Hume's empiricism was expressed thus: "a wise man proportions his belief according to the evidence". He adds that the evidence for the miracle would have to be so persuasive and strong to overthrow the evidence that supports the existence of natural laws, which is considerable. As he notes, "no testimony is sufficient to establish a miracle unless the testimony be of such a kind, that its falsehood would be more miraculous, than the fact which it endeavours to establish". He went on to say that no such evidence for miracles exists which would allow us to suspend our understanding that natural laws are not broken, and that it would be "irrational to believe the highly improbable as this is to believe against the evidence". (**WILKINSON** and **CAMPBELL**) The balance of probability is against the miracle having taken place.

3. Now that such probability has been established by the appeal to empirical evidence, Hume looks at the event itself and those who witnessed it. When he looks at the quality of the witnesses to the supposed miracles, Hume notes that they are not of sufficient quality to give us reason to believe their reports - there is not "a sufficient number of men, of such unquestioned good sense, education and learning, as to secure us against all delusion in themselves".

4. Hume further argues that we are so prone to want to believe in the unusual, and that a miracle has happened, that this is

sometimes the reason we believe such has actually happened; those within religion who know that a miracle did not happen continue to tell the story that it did in order to aid the spread of their faith.

5. Hume then argues that miracle stories take place in "ignorant and barbarous nations" which have not been enlightened by reason nor follow the sceptic's requirement for empirical evidence.

6. The fact that different religions make truth claims and back up those claims with miracles cancels all miracles out, argues Hume. As **JACKSON** explains, "the differing claims of the many religions result in them being mutually exclusive. Miracles are often presented as proof to the claims of religious belief, but if beliefs differ so much from one religion to another, then it only results in claims cancelling each other out".

RESPONSES TO HUME

1. Hume seems to be working with a model of natural laws in which those laws are more fixed and unalterable than is actually the case; this model would discount many advances in science where laws have been seen to be clarified or changed by exceptions to those laws. Laws are descriptive, not prescriptive, and likely to change as understanding increases. **SWINBURNE** argued that a law of nature "is the best description of how the world works that we currently have", **(TAYLOR)** but which could be modified through a new discovery. Natural laws are **PROBABILISTIC**, not deterministic.

2. What does Hume mean by "people of sufficient number and education" being required to witness a miracle? How many would need to testify to the event taking place? What level of education is required before they can be believed? What would Hume say to modern-day claims to miracles, such as those that have been studied carefully by medical practitioners at Lourdes? **VARDY** argues that Hume's criticisms only apply to the quality of the witnesses to a miracle. What would Hume think if a miracle happened to him?

3. In reference to Hume's wider work many have pointed out the logical **PROBLEM OF INDUCTION** - indeed, Hume was well aware of this himself. Induction is only true if the principle behind induction is true, or as **WILKINSON** and **CAMPBELL** write, "the only proof we have that many instances of events giving us probable general conclusions is the many instances of events giving us probable general conclusions". It is questionable then if this principle can be used to discount the occurrence of miracles; what if miracles are the exception to the inductive instances and that instead of induction predicting an exact future, it just predicts probabilities? Although most but not all testimony may support the uniformity of natural laws, miracles could still occasionally (by their nature they are occasional/unusual) take place. The least we can say is that the problem of induction leaves the door open to examples which go against previous instances of natural laws, however numerous observed repetitions of those laws there are.

4. Following on from the above, why would the improbability of the event mean that it did not or could never happen? There are many things which are most unlikely that take place where the balance of probability was stacked against that event occurring.

AHLUWALIA wonders if Hume is guilty of making a "jump from what is improbable to what is beyond rational acceptance". Believers might say that precisely because it is improbable it is more likely that God has intervened in nature. God may, as **POLKINGHORNE** notes, act in new and unexpected ways as a situation demands. Or, as **SWINBURNE** notes, because laws are probabilistic and not fixed, there could be events that take place that are unlikely, but don't actually break the laws of nature.

5. Why do miracles in different religions cancel each other out? **SWINBURNE** claims this would only be the case if they were incompatible with one another.

6. **SWINBURNE** (for whom the principle of credulity and the principle of testimony would also be relevant in the case of miracle), argues that we gain our knowledge of miracles from memory, the testimony of others and the physical traces left behind after an event (for example, the grave clothes of Christ in the tomb). These are the three types of evidence used for scientific laws; he concludes therefore that "if the evidence is not sufficient to establish the occurrence of a miracle then neither is it sufficient to establish the certainty of a natural law". Hume famously rejected accounts of miracles that had been experienced at the grave of Abbe Paris, a well-known Jesuit, despite these being witnessed by credible and reputable people. When Hume notes that we must reject these accounts because we have to oppose the "cloud of witnesses" with the "absolute impossibility or miraculous nature of the events to which they relate", is he judging the case before he looks at the **EMPIRICAL** evidence?

DEFINITION 2: CREATION ACTIVITY

In God's Action in the World, **WILES** moved away from Hume's idea, which expressed a traditional understanding of miracles as one-off events at the will of a deity. He attempted to broaden the understanding of miracle, arguing that this is compatible with the ideas of early Christians, who, notes **AHLUWALIA**, saw "creation itself and all the regularities of the working of nature [as] entirely dependent on the will of God". In Wiles' view, God's action in creating the world should be understood as much broader than one-off events where God has suddenly intervened in a situation. Rather, as he notes, "the idea of divine action should be in relation to the world as a whole".

The idea of God intervening occasionally and randomly in the world is not impossible scientifically or on rational grounds for Wiles; God could do this, but it would have to be infrequently otherwise the laws of nature would no longer be laws that held in the majority of cases. However, this traditional view of miracles is not defensible from a **MORAL** standpoint for Wiles, as there are just too many times when God doesn't intervene, such as in the horrors of the concentration camps. This lack of intervention on occasions and his action at some other, more trivial times, makes God very **ARBITRARY** and not worthy of worship. To heal someone's bad back and yet not stop terrible events such as an earthquake killing thousands is not morally or theologically defensible; however, viewing the creation and sustaining of the whole of the world as the single way in which God has acted gets over this difficulty raised by the traditional, and Humean, view of miracles, and in doing so helps Christians defend the concept of miracle in the face of evil. "Underlying all of [Wiles'] work is a very lively awareness of the presence of God behind the world, performing a single miracle of creation." (**WILKINSON** and **CAMPBELL**)

Furthermore, Wiles suggested that the interventionist-type miracles, such as the virgin birth, are not actually essential for the Christian faith in the way in which they have been portrayed, and that faithfulness to Christ without the need for dramatic signs or interventions was actually what Christ himself stressed. Wiles argues that the meaning, not the process, of the "miracle" is what is important, and the lack of historical verification for the actual miracles, as direct interventions of God, does not matter if they are **SYMBOLICALLY** understood.

Responses to Wiles

1. **SWINBURNE** responds to Wiles by saying that a loving parent would actually bend the rules in response to pleading by their children, but would not do this too often as it would take away responsibility the child bears for their actions. Wiles' idea of miracle changes the traditional understanding of God's nature, which is of a being who is loving, powerful and responsive to his creation.

2. What would be the purpose of praying if God will not intervene in specific situations? Wiles' view goes against much of Christian tradition and understanding; even though the reasons why God does not seem to intervene in some situations but does so in others, does mystify Christians, they would not be willing to give up the belief that God does intervene. The biblical picture does seem to suggest a God who intervenes in human history, which would be the view held by **THEISTS**, as opposed to **DEISTS**, (see key words) which Wiles might be. However, **EYRE** et al note that maybe Wiles changes the idea of prayer from being viewed as a long list of things which a person would like God to fix, to "allowing an individual to connect with God's will".

3. Has Wiles attempted to rationalise the actions of God in human terms? Whilst many Christians find it difficult to see why God doesn't seem to intervene in certain situations, this might be precisely because it is God who is acting and not a human being acting according to human reason. Wiles perhaps missed the point of miracles, which are to **REVEAL SOMETHING OF THE NATURE OF GOD** rather than just to rescue people? "A comparatively small miracle might be more significant because of what it shows of God." **(AHLUWALIA)**

4. **CASE STUDY** - There have been recent reports of gold dust and jewels appearing when Christians are gathered together to worship God. These jewels have reportedly been examined by jewellers, who are impressed by their purity, yet perplexed as to what they are. Furthermore, there are a number of people who claim to have been given gold fillings (see the Darren Wilson film "Finger of God", Wanderlust Productions). These seem such trivial miracles to perform today, when Christians in Syria are fearing for their lives. The response given by Christians in the film is that such occurrences reveal something of God's character; he is gracious, playful, and responds to his children's child-like faith. (Mark 10:13-16)

DEFINITION 3: IMPROBABILITY

Miracles are extraordinary coincidences, in which no laws of nature are broken, but where events happen together in a most unlikely manner. The person witnessing these events interprets them as miracles. **HOLLAND** tells the story of how a train stops just before it hits a boy who was on the track. His mother, looking on, horrified, interprets the train stopping as a miracle, whereas when the event was investigated, it was discovered that the driver had collapsed at the wheel and an automatic brake had been applied. The mother still thinks that a miracle has taken place. **HUME** rejects this because no law of nature has been broken, and there will be other times when the train does not stop and a child does, unfortunately, get hit. It is questionable if Holland's account is what people belonging to a religion understand as miracle.

Miracles are also **REVELATORY**. For a believer a miracle or miracle story might be interpreted as signs:

- **AUTHORITY** of God over nature

- **FORETASTE** of the day God's will is fulfilled

- **EVIDENCE** that Jesus is divine - a **CREATOR** and **REDEEMER**

- **EVIDENCE** of God's continuing care for the world

These signs depend on the interpretation of the person who witnesses or reads about them, and maybe miracles are meant to be understood by those who already have faith, not as something that is supposed to make someone have faith. Jesus' miracles have significance because they reveal something of the nature of God, which is why he refuses to do them "on demand" in the way that "magicians" of his day did unusual things to impress the crowds. The New Testament does not use the word "miracle" but **DUNAMIS**, meaning "power" or **SEMEION**, meaning a "sign of God", and this might be a better way of reading events such as the resurrection as signs of the power of God which reveal his nature.

In the Old Testament, **TAYLOR** remarks that people did not understand the world as one which was governed by natural laws, but one where the activity of God was seen through his "power and involvement with the world." In **JOSHUA 10** God stops the sun in the sky for 24 hours in order for the Israelites to win a battle and this fits with the power and involvement of God in the world as opposed to a suspension of natural law. As **TAYLOR** notes, "it is perhaps incorrect to see the miracles of the Bible as violating natural laws ... because the stories, particularly those in the Jewish Scriptures [Old Testament], come from a culture lacking any idea about laws of nature". God battles on behalf of his people to achieve his will and purposes for them, and the people gain this underlying meaning from the event.

MIRACLES AND THE PROBLEM OF EVIL

Here we ask a number of questions which can be linked particularly to **HUME, SWINBURNE** and **WILES**; what particular problems are raised by the occurrence of miracles?

1. Is God arbitrary and unfair? Traditional understandings of miracles (and the definition **HUME** uses) as interventions of God may raise the difficult idea that God is partisan, ie someone who is not fair and biased towards certain situations. Yet this undermines the Judeao-Christian definition of God (see Ephesians 6, "there is no favouritism with God"). This is a moral and theological problem, as evil seems to be allowed in some circumstances where people have cried out for God to intervene. **WILES** recognises, and thinks he solves, this issue, but it is for you to evaluate if he has done so at the cost of Orthodox Christian understanding of miracle.

2. Does the world have to be a place of hardship and suffering for us to grow, as **HICK** implies? If God did keep intervening through miracles, would that be like a parent who never actually allows their child to experience many of the potentially lovely and good things of life because those things can only be learnt through some painful experience, for example the process of learning to ride a bike. Link with **IRENAEUS' THEODICY** in the Problem of Evil section.

3. If God always intervenes how could we have **PERSONAL RESPONSIBILITY** for our choices? And how would such an interventionist God show any respect for human freedom? Furthermore, the world's natural processes cause earthquakes and tsunamis - should God keep intervening in such processes

when they are part of a delicate balance for how the world works? For every day there is a tsunami there are many when there are not, for which God is not thanked; if people were being "fair" towards God perhaps blaming God for a tsunami should be balanced by thanks when one doesn't happen.

4. Should miracles be seen as **SYMBOLS** which carry deep meaning rather than literal events where natural laws are overcome? If they are, would this get round the problems that **WILES** raises and problems concerning evil and suffering?

5. How would we know if God had intervened to stop evil if that evil did not occur? Parents can often see obstacles ahead when a child is learning to walk which they remove. The child did not see the parent remove the obstacle.

Key quotes

1. "A miracle is a violation of the laws of nature." Hume

2. "The gazing populace receive greedily, without examination, whatever soothes superstition, and promotes wonder." Hume

3. "Some people have suggested that stories such as Moses leading the Israelites across the Red Sea could be an example of God violating the laws of nature, but equally the sea and weather all combining to cause this great flood could be explained in natural terms." Taylor

4. "Where some had probably already had enough to drink, but do nothing to free the Jews from Roman rule? ... why make a statue drink, but do nothing for the hungry and persecuted in Darfur?" Wilkinson and Campbell

5. "The same event, described by the theist as 'a miracle', rationalised by the scientist as a 'probability of very low likelihood', may be reconciled by the philosopher as an impossible event that may have a divine cause if the divine exists." Phelan

6. "On the whole, Hume's scepticism is shown to be not so much destructive as pragmatic when applied to a real philosophical case study." Phelan

7. "It would seem strange that no miraculous intervention prevented Auschwitz or Hiroshima while the purposes apparently forwarded by some of the miracles acclaimed in traditional Christian faith seem trivial by comparison." Wiles

Confusions to avoid

- Work carefully with the definitions of the scholars. Read their views thoroughly, as scholars such as Hume, Swinburne and Wiles differ widely in what they understand to be a miracle, and critique of these views will be more successful if you have understood their positions clearly. If the understanding of different definitions is in place, it gives you more chance to analyse different examples of miracles clearly; it is better if you are able to work with some examples rather than talk about miracles in general. Hume, Wiles and Swinburne would have a different take on the same event, purely because of their different definitions which act as their starting positions.

- The syllabus warns against turning the philosophical issue of miracles into a biblical studies essay. Although you may make reference to relevant examples and quotations from theologians, the Bible (or other holy book), and the Church, be careful to keep your focus on philosophical contributors and debates by emphasising the characteristics of God, or other philosophical debates about miracles.

GET MORE HELP

Get more help with miracles by using the links below:

http://i-pu.sh/C7D36W99

The Problem of Evil

KEY TERMS

- **EPISTEMIC DISTANCE** - distance from knowledge of God.

- **ESCHATOLOGICAL** - normally referring to the end times, or the end of history; in Hick's theory it refers to post-death.

- **MORAL EVIL** - intentional actions by humans which cause suffering.

- **NATURAL EVIL** - events in nature which result in suffering.

- **OMNIBENEVOLENT** - literally "all good"; God, a being who is all-good or loving.

- **OMNIPOTENT** - literally "all power"; God having the characteristic of being all-powerful.

- **OMNISCIENT** - literally "all knowledge"; God knowing all things, including future events.

- **PRIVATIO BONI** - the privation of good; evil is not a substance or entity but the privation, or lack, of good.

- **THEODICY** - literally, theos (God), diké (justice); an attempt to justify the existence of God in the face of the existence of evil and suffering. In particular the attempt to defend the existence of a God with the attributes of omnipotence and omnibenevolence.

The arguments studied so far may have seemed very theoretical and not always related to the reality of our existence. The challenge to the belief in a good and powerful God which is presented here is far more personal and relates to the sometimes painful and anguished **EXPERIENCE** of being alive and aware that there is suffering in the world. However, whilst this is true and the argument concerns real and evidential evil and suffering, do not let emotion cloud your responses to this issue.

WHAT DO WE MEAN BY EVIL?

Scholars have classically divided evil into two types, though in reality there are many links between these types and the distinction between the two is not always easy to delineate (for example, think about an event such as a flood following heavy rain; this would seem like a natural event, but might actually have been caused, or made much worse, by deforestation carried out by man). The two types are:

- **MORAL EVIL** - This term is used to denote evil actions committed by human beings, such as rape, murder and war, as well as actions which result in psychological and mental pain. These actions are freely committed and result in suffering, sometimes on a mass scale. There are countless accounts of atrocities that show the depth of human cruelty, including modern day examples.

- **NATURAL EVIL** - This term refers to events in nature that cause suffering, and which are not directly the result of human action, such as earthquakes and hurricanes. There are countless examples of the devastation that natural events cause, where thousands of lives are lost and habitats destroyed in a very short space of time. Disease and illness would also come under the title of natural evil. Philosophers disagree as to whether such "natural" events should be called "evil".

The issue at stake in this argument is the challenge such events present to the belief in a good and powerful God, who is not only held to have created the world with such regular and devastating natural disasters, illnesses and diseases present in it but who seems to allow such to continue to take place.

THE PROBLEM

- If God is all-good he would not allow moral and natural evil to exist. Having a **BENEVOLENT** nature, he would have the motivation to abolish evil.

- If God was all-powerful, he would be able to stop evil. Having an **OMNIPOTENT** nature, he would have the ability to eliminate it entirely.

- And yet **EVIL EXISTS**.

Within the Judaeo-Christian tradition, God is also believed to be **OMNISCIENT** (although this is often included as an element of omnipotence). Omniscience raises further issues because it would imply that God knows that evil is going to happen but does not prevent it from doing so. The subject studied earlier in this guide concerning the nature of God as the **CREATOR** is also relevant here; if God created everything in the universe ex nihilo then the question needs to be asked if God created evil.

Earlier arguments concerning whether the universe has an ultimate purpose and meaning also come into play. A **THEODICY** attempts to reach a "big picture" conclusion about a reason why things exist (including the possibility of a "purpose" for the existence of evil), whereas many think such a search for overarching reason and meaning is both futile and unnecessary. Indeed, Russell finds the idea of the world as accident more plausible than the world as a **PURPOSEFUL** work of a God.

On the evidence of the immense amount of suffering in the world, Russell states that the most fitting description of God, if he existed, would be "a fiend".

A key question is how can an all-loving and all-powerful God tolerate one incident of suffering in his creation? Is there a solution to this problem which maintains God's character as understood in classical Theism even in the face of evil, or, as **HUME** suggests, does one of these attributes of God have to be removed to solve the inconsistency?

The attempt to justify the existence of God in the face of evil and suffering is called a **THEODICY**. Whilst some scholars such as **RUBENSTEIN** say that it is impossible to frame a theodicy after the horrors of Auschwitz, those that are formulated normally attempt to:

- blame a source other than God for the existence of evil, or

- say why evil is justified or even necessary for a greater good, or

- reinterpret (without removing) what is meant by omnibenevolence and omnipotence.

Few theodicies take the line that evil does not exist, but **AUGUSTINE** does conclude that evil is not a substance as such, as explained below.

THE THEODICY OF AUGUSTINE

AUGUSTINE'S THEODICY continues to have influence upon Christian thought, 15 centuries after it was written. We can take his argument step by step:

Augustine's opening premise was that God, who is perfect, and therefore all-powerful and all-loving, made a good world. He based this understanding on the teaching of **GENESIS**, where God declared that his creation was good at the end of each of the first five days and very good at the end of the sixth. The universe, with a **HIERARCHY OF BEINGS** from God down to angels, humans and the rest of creation, was ordered and in harmony.

However, after the creation of a good universe, both angels and man fell. The **FALL OF ADAM AND EVE** is outlined in Genesis. Augustine argued that they clearly **FREELY CHOSE TO DISOBEY GOD**. They chose not to do what is good and rejected what God had told them to do and in so doing chose "non-being" material things rather than the fullness of their being, God. Hence, by their **ORIGINAL SIN** of disobedience to God's instructions, Adam and Eve introduced a break and discord between them and their creator, God. Humanity **FELL** from a close relationship with God.

This "choosing of evil" was actually choosing to not live up to the standard of goodness that God intended; because it was choosing not to do that which is good, it is a **PRIVATION**. By this, Augustine meant that **EVIL IS THE LACK OF GOODNESS**, like blindness is the lack of sight. To stress, evil, in Augustine's theodicy, is not a **SUBSTANCE**, but the lack of good. In Latin, the phrase is **PRIVATIO BONI**. We can think about this idea of privation using many examples - cold is the absence of heat, ill health the absence of health etc - and these things only have understanding in relation to what they lack. Adam and Eve now lack "right order" and harmony with God - they have chosen to be **DEPRIVED**.

The idea of **LACK** is very important, but be careful. It is not evil that a stone lacks the ability to talk, or a worm lacks the ability to walk. These are qualities that the stone and the worm lack, but because they lack them they are not evil. However, when man chooses to not "hit the mark" (this is what "to sin" means), he is evil in the sense that he fails to live up to his morally good and God-given nature. And the choice to do this is due to our **FREE WILL** and hence, carries with it **RESPONSIBILITY**. If someone cannot use their arm due to an accident, they lack the health of the arm, but they cannot help this, unlike the lack of kindness we show when we are cruel to someone. On this point **TAYLOR** writes:

> "According to Augustine's view, if you say that a human being is evil, or that their actions are evil, you are saying that the way they behave does not match expectations about how a human being should behave. For example, if you racially abuse people, rob or torture them, you are not living up to the standards expected of human beings. It is the failure to be what you should be that is wrong."

Evil therefore comes about because of Adam and Eve's **FREE MORAL CHOICE**. Adam and Eve, when tempted by **LUCIFER**, use their free will to not live to the standards for which they were created, and through this disobedience, evil enters the world; as noted, evil here is not as a substance in itself, but the lack of goodness. Both moral and natural evil stem from the wrong moral choices made. Pain in childbirth and hard work making the soil productive are both immediate results listed in **GENESIS 3**. **MORAL EVIL** comes through Adam and Eve's choice, which sets them at a distance from God; **NATURAL EVIL** is due to the balance of nature being upset and the work of the fallen angel **LUCIFER**, who tries to be more powerful than God, bringing discord to nature which results in suffering. But **AUGUSTINE** argued that free will is a good thing in itself as it enables good and right choices to be made and is worth the price of evil occurring. Of course, if God is perfect, he would have known humanity would make a wrong choice and fall, but he chose for humans to have free will so that they could freely love him rather than be robots without choice.

AUGUSTINE argued that the goodness of the world is seen clearly when people choose to do good as it stands in contrast to when people do evil and misuse their free will, just as "a dash of black makes the colours in a painting stand out". (**PHELAN**) This is known as the **AESTHETIC PRINCIPLE**; as Augustine writes:

> "In the universe, even that which is called evil, when it is regulated and put in its own place, only enhances our admiration of the good; for we enjoy and value the good more when we compare it with the evil."

God did not create anything **IMPERFECT**; he could not therefore have created evil, thus, evil is not a "thing". Neither is God in a **BATTLE** between the forces of good and evil - spiritual forces at war might make people not responsible for their choices, and **AUGUSTINE** stressed human responsibility stemmed from humans being free to choose. But be careful not to say that Augustine denied that evil existed; it "exists" not as a separate "thing", because God would have had to have made it if it was a thing, but evil exists as a **LACK OF GOODNESS**. Indeed, later Augustine goes on to say that evil comes from God due to the fact that he keeps human beings in existence, and they are beings who have this free choice to become evil.

Now Augustine has established that Adam and Eve's choice gives birth to evil, how does he account for ongoing evil in the world? As all humanity is descended from Adam and Eve, then all humans inherit their **SINFUL NATURE**, which chooses to live in rebellion towards, and in discord with, God, and not reach the standard for which God created us. Augustine says that humans are **SEMINALLY PRESENT** in Adam, and, as such, our punishment is deserved.

For Augustine, "all evil is either sin or punishment for sin".

However, Christ is the **SECOND ADAM** who shows God's grace and mercy in offering humanity a chance to restore its relationship with God and avert hell, which would be just punishment for sin.

Key steps

1. Creation is perfect; God is all-powerful and all-loving.

2. Adam and Eve have free choice - a good thing.

3. They, and Satan, freely chose not to do good - **PRIVATIO BONI** (the Fall). God does not create evil.

4. Humans and angels are responsible for this choice which brings moral and natural evil into the world, resulting in suffering.

5. The goodness in the world as a whole can clearly be seen when contrasted with when people choose the privatio boni. God keeps in existence people who have freedom to choose not to be good.

6. The sinful nature of Adam is present in humans.

7. Jesus offers a way for human nature to be restored.

STRENGTHS

- It could be argued that the **DEFAULT POSITION OF HUMANITY IS GOOD**, in that we are offended when people do harm; news reports are full of things which go against our expectations, such as murder and conflict, and this is why they are news. Is this a hint that the world is "good", as Augustine suggested, and that evil is a privation of that goodness? Do we feel that the world is "out of balance", which is why there are so many attempts to help those who are less fortunate than ourselves or who suffer through the effects of natural disasters? Is this better than any evolutionary explanation there might be for trying to preserve the weak?

- The idea of **EVIL LACKING SUBSTANCE** can make **LOGICAL SENSE**, just like darkness being the absence of light, and cold the absence of heat, are logically coherent ideas. **LAW** has recently challenged this idea however, and said that from the clues in the universe, God might in fact be evil; such a God just puts some good in the world to let people think he is good. He argues that the idea that "God is evil" can be supported from the world with as much credence as the idea that "God is good".

- If **FREEDOM AND RESPONSIBILITY** is to be genuine, then our choices have to have consequences, otherwise it does not matter what we choose to do. It has been argued that this is the type of freedom we seem to experience and which is at the heart of **AUGUSTINE'S** theodicy. The alternative to unrestricted moral freedom seems to suggest something less than what it means to be human.

- The idea of freedom and interpretation of the ideas at the heart of Augustine's theodicy does not depend on a **LITERAL** reading of Genesis. Many Christians regard the meaning found in the Genesis story of moral and natural evil reflecting an accurate reading of the human condition and humanity's free response towards God and how we act in creation.

WEAKNESSES

- Does our **EXPERIENCE** agree with the idea that evil is simply the lack of good? To those who have been victims of rape or violence, or genocide on a mass scale, there seems to be more than the **PRIVATIO BONI** at work. It does not seem that the careful planning, organisation and implementation of shockingly cruel and depraved acts which were part of the Holocaust can be explained by thousands of people just lacking the good.

- Does Augustine's theory explain **WHY** angels and humans should choose to not obey God? It would seem that this even stumped Augustine; concerning why the will should be turned not to do the right thing, he said, somewhat surprisingly, "let no one, then, seek to know from me what I know that I do not know".

- Giedrius **SAULYTIS** writes that according to Augustine, "to seek the causes of this defection is as if someone sought to see darkness, or hear silence. Thus, the problem of evil is wrapped up in mystery", other than that created things, "have within them the tendency toward non-existence" (which is to choose against their good and become corrupted and deprived).

- If Augustine does not know the **ULTIMATE CAUSE AND REASON FOR EVIL** and why humanity wills to do it, of what use is his theodicy as an explanation?

- Following on from the above point, God's goodness can be questioned if the whole system is set up in a way that allows for such suffering on a massive scale. Schleiermacher has pointed out the **LOGICAL CONTRADICTION** in the idea that a perfect world could go wrong. And how could such a world go wrong if there was no knowledge of evil for humanity to choose at the Fall?

- Despite the offer of God's grace in the form of Christ, is it a loving God who keeps a system going in which every successive generation after Adam (including, for Augustine, babies) is punished for original sin? Not only is this a problem as far as the **JUST NATURE** of God is concerned, but biologically each human being is not descended from Adam. That being the case, in what sense can the idea that we are "seminally present in the loins of Adam" work? Scientific understanding would also question the whole underlying source of Augustine's theodicy, including Adam and Eve and an **ACTUAL FALL** of man, which, despite claims otherwise, might still require a literal reading of Genesis. **EVOLUTION** through natural selection over time to the stage of rational human beings, lies in contrast to the Genesis reading which starts with a perfect world and a humanity that falls away from a blissful state.

- Many, such as **DOSTOYEVSKY**, have questioned the idea of a loving God based on the sheer amount of suffering in the world, even if it allows humans to be free; is God's loving gift of freedom worth this cost? It would be difficult to quantify how much suffering is too much; should toothache not be allowed for example? Others have questioned how a good God could conceive of the existence of a punishment such as **HELL**.

THE THEODICY OF IRENAEUS

While Augustine's theodicy is sometimes called a **SOUL-DECIDING THEODICY**, as we choose/decide what we will do with the good gift of free will, **IRENAEUS'** argument is known as a **SOUL-MAKING THEODICY**. It has within it a very different idea of the source of evil. Writing 200 years before Augustine, Irenaeus' theodicy works in the following way:

1. Irenaeus read the **GENESIS** creation account **LITERALLY**. From this basis he argued that God desires for humanity to reach **PERFECTION**, but that this perfection is something to be reached from an initial state of imperfection (this is different to Augustine's belief of humans falling away from perfection). Humans are created **IMMATURE**, but can progress towards maturity and perfection. Irenaeus worked with the teaching of **GENESIS 1** verse 26, where humans were made in the **IMAGE** of God, but were to develop into the **LIKENESS** of God.

2. It is important to unpack this idea. **COLE** notes that this is a move from the "form" (image) of God to the content (likeness) of God. The Good News translation of the Bible uses the words "they (people) will be like us (God) and resemble us". **TAYLOR** et al note that Irenaeus understands "like us" as God creating people with "intelligence, morality and a personality" and the state of "resembling" God as peoples' souls growing "until they resembled the very nature of God".

3. Being child-like, humans make **MISTAKES** and do things which are not wise, but this is a result of both their lack of maturity and the **FREEDOM** they have. In Genesis chapter 3, Adam and Eve are exiled (through an actual event known as the Fall), from the

Garden of Eden to make the journey towards God's likeness in a world which is suited for them to make such a pilgrimage. Whilst they do bear some responsibility for their choices against God's commands, **IRENAEUS** held that the serpent who tricked them is to blame. Adam and Eve are banished from the garden, but this is not punishment in the Augustine sense; **TAYLOR** notes that such punishment is offered in the way children are set boundaries, and it is therefore "educative". Neither is the Fall as catastrophic for **IRENAEUS** as it is for **AUGUSTINE**, as it is a mistake which is part of the human experience of growing up, rather than a movement away from perfection, and there certainly is no sense of **ORIGINAL SIN** in Irenaeus' theodicy, unlike there is in Augustine's.

4. In the playground of this world, humanity can develop, and grow towards "good". Evil and suffering provide **TESTS** for that growth but humans can make moral progress in the world as they journey. Irenaeus noted that in the Bible there were many people, such as **JONAH**, who went through suffering in order to grow, make mistakes, learn the need to repent and fulfil the purposes God had for them. How we react to this suffering is the key. And **JESUS**, through suffering, restores the damage that Adam has done by his choice and makes it possible for there to be union between God and man again. Jesus rescues those taken captive by the serpent by taking Adam's sin on the cross, restoring friendship between God and man.

Thus, **EVIL IS NECESSARY** as an essential part of the environment in which humanity can grow, in which we can choose to live above our basic animal instincts. God, who is all-good and all-powerful, allows evil and suffering as part of the environment in which the journey from imperfection to perfection takes place and therefore there is purpose for both good and evil within the creation of the universe. (This is very different from **AUGUSTINE'S** explanation of evil). Evil and suffering are necessary in order to help us develop **MORAL VIRTUE** and maturity, to grow in character to resemble God, and be good like him, eventually achieving perfection. Without suffering and the prospect of death, there is no testing which provides opportunity for growth and repentance and learning of what is good; neither would there be any contrast between what is good and what is evil (see the aesthetic principle). For Irenaeus evil is not a privation, but a very real and necessary part of the world in which we develop towards maturity. If so, does this offer a possible philosophical answer to the problem of evil?

Because the world is like this, it is what **HICK** calls a **VALE OF SOUL-MAKING**. Our souls can choose to live towards ourselves or towards God, to develop kindness and empathy and to learn from our mistakes. Being created perfect would not have given us the opportunity to develop and learn. This growth requires a determination of the will within the reality that the choices we make with our free will have consequences. Expecting to be bailed out every time we make an error would not develop our souls and would compromise genuine free will.

The journey **CONTINUES AFTER DEATH** because the soul carries on its journey until ready to enter heaven; it is important, however, to note that for Irenaeus those who continue to reject God and who do not grow will face punishment post death.

HICK has developed Irenaeus' ideas to argue that humanity is able to make this evolutionary journey towards a relationship with God. He argues that in this world humanity is at an **EPISTEMIC DISTANCE** from God, meaning at a distance of knowing God, and can, through free choice, make a journey towards God, developing goodness in the face of a world which contains evil and disasters. The world seems to be one which is entirely suited to enable soul-making to go on. Indeed, our **RESPONSE** to catastrophic events can potentially help to **DEVELOP CHARACTER** traits such as empathy, kindness and compassion. Humans have the knowledge of the laws of nature in which they can explore the world, but it is precisely those predictable and regular **LAWS OF NATURE** which govern the fact that earthquakes and hurricanes exist, or bricks remain hard (and do not suddenly by some divine intervention become soft) when they fall on someone's head. In addition to this, because of the fact that we are truly free, we can cause suffering, or have pain inflicted on us. **HICK** argues that without the possibility of these dangers, **NO PROGRESS WOULD BE MADE** either within the soul of a person or in any area of life such as the arts or the sciences, and in a world of no suffering, nothing actually would ever be seen as right or wrong. No real virtues would develop when we act kindly without the possibility of us not choosing this path and acting maliciously.

This process through suffering makes the soul (although you could argue that for **DOSTOYEVSKY** this very process crushes the soul). Hick differs from Irenaeus by suggesting that eventually everyone will be able to enter into a relationship with God post death as only **UNIVERSAL SALVATION**, which completes the making of everyone's soul, fully satisfies the purpose of God allowing evil and suffering in this world. Because Hick suggests that the pain of this world has an ultimate answer post death, his approach is **ESCHATOLOGICAL**.

THE FREE WILL DEFENCE

Central to the theodicies of **AUGUSTINE, IRENAEUS** and **HICK** is the idea that there has to be evil and suffering in the world if humans are to be genuinely free; we have to have **THE POSSIBILITY OF CHOOSING WRONG**, with the **REAL CONSEQUENCES** of those choices, in order for us to be **TRULY FREE**.

For Augustine, the choice made when humanity misused free will resulted in evil which is taken on the cross by Christ. For Irenaeus the free will to choose is part of our soul's development towards the likeness of God.

Is this freedom worth the cost? What are the alternatives? **MACKIE** suggests that God could have made a world in which humans always choose what is good, but many have rejected this as not what is meant by freedom. Others have suggested that perhaps our choices could result in less suffering than they seem to in this world. Others question whether a God of love should have made such a world at all.

STRENGTHS

- Does part of what it means to be human and **GENUINELY FREE** necessarily involve the possibility of choosing good and evil? Irenaeus argued that for a person to have any less a choice would mean he is no longer human. What would it mean for human identity if freedom wasn't genuine and there weren't good and bad choices to be made?

- Could the development of humanity really have happened **WITHOUT RISK** or danger or difficulty? Would virtuous choices develop if we did not have **ALTERNATIVE CHOICES** that we could make? Would we progress if God intervened all the time rather than letting us learn from our mistakes? Is it better and **MORE LOVING** parenting to set boundaries (laws of nature), but allow freedom within those boundaries and encourage (rather than dictate) good choices? Do we sometimes work on the principle that some suffering is indeed worth the end result? If so, is it possible to translate that principle to a cosmic level?

- **POST-DEATH** resolution of the problem of suffering might indeed be a way of fulfilling God's purpose for people to move from being in God's image to his likeness. It would suggest that for those who suffer unimaginable pain in this life, the whole journey is **NOT FUTILE**, which, if this life was all there was, it might seem to be. Is it possible to offer alternative hope if there is no life after death?

WEAKNESSES

- It is difficult to understand why there needs to be the **EXTREME AMOUNT** of suffering in the world for humans to learn. After a certain amount of pain, the human soul might actually fail to learn its lesson. For children born into extreme poverty, involving malnutrition, to suggest the idea of suffering as a soul-making journey could seem almost immoral. If, further to that, such children are to continue their journey of soul-making in the afterlife (what does this mean - that they would suffer further, post death, in order to learn and develop more?), would this seem fair or loving in any way? In reference to this idea, suffering seems to be so randomly allocated.

- **PHILLIPS** questions how a **GOD OF LOVE** can **JUSTIFY SUFFERING** to fulfil his purposes. He is particularly critical of viewing a kind response to the suffering of others as a way of developing one's soul; it would almost suggest that people should look for the suffering of others and, in a way, be grateful for it as it gives them a chance to respond kindly and develop their character. Using suffering as a means to justify the end (**INSTRUMENTALISM**) of moral development is an example of a case where a theodicy adds to the problem of evil rather than solves it. Could there be alternative pain-free ways to develop the soul?

- How strong and philosophically valid is any theory that relies on post-death existence for its solution? Is the theodicy more likely to be accepted on **THEOLOGICAL** grounds by a believer than **PHILOSOPHICAL** grounds by an atheist?

PROCESS THEOLOGY

A modern solution to the problem of evil is **PROCESS THEOLOGY**. This idea was postulated by **AN WHITEHEAD** and developed by **GRIFFIN**. They suggest that God is not omnipotent and did not create the universe but is bound by its natural laws. God's role in the universe was to start the evolutionary process and he is now **POWERLESS** to stop the evil that is occurring. Since God is part of the universe he also suffers when evil occurs; but despite this he is to blame for evil because he started a process which he knew he would be unable to control. This idea was postulated by **AN WHITEHEAD** and developed by **GRIFFIN**. These two philosophers seek to justify the evil in the world by believing the universe has produced enough good to outweigh the evil that occurs.

CRITIQUE

Some philosophers have doubted whether it is a theodicy at all, since it actually denies that God is all-powerful in the first place and as such, it **FAILS TO KEEP GOD'S CHARACTER INTACT**. As it denies that God is omnipotent, it also brings into question whether such a limited God is actually a being **WORTHY OF WORSHIP**. A final criticism is that while good has outweighed the evil in the world, this is still of **LITTLE COMFORT** to those who have actually suffered, and since there is no promise of heaven, there is no certainty that the innocent will be rewarded.

FURTHER CONSIDERATIONS

AUGUSTINE tried to move away from the idea of evil being "God's fault", whilst Irenaeus argued that evil could serve a purpose. In general, when writing about the "fault" idea, students should be careful. It could be useful to hold the "God's fault" argument in **BALANCE**. If God is blamed when an earthquake takes place, is it logical to thank him when one doesn't? If God is blamed for seemingly faulty features of the universe, is it consistent to thank him for beauty and laws of nature that mean, for example, trees grow and produce fruit? What would Augustine and **IRENAEUS** say about the "balance of blame and thanks"?

How does one classify illnesses such as cancer? If cancer occurs as a direct result of smoking, is **GOD** to be held **RESPONSIBLE** for the very possibility of the occurrence of cancer in the person, or is the smoker responsible for misusing their freedom, knowing the possible consequences? Could there be a world in which we could do what we like without bad side effects or would this not be what we mean by human existence? Is God's **OMNIPOTENCE** limited by logical possibilities, so that this type of world would be a logical contradiction, or, as **DESCARTES** argued, does God's omnipotence mean that he must be able to do anything and not be limited to what is logically possible? **BRAND** has written extensively on the idea that pain is God's gift to the world as without its use as a barrier on our actions, we would suffer even more. Further, he notes that the same sensitivity that withdraws fingers when placed on something sharp is precisely the same preciseness of touch needed to play the piano softly. However, **HEBBLETHWAITE**, in **AHLUWALIA**, writes:

> *"Part of the problem of evil is the fact that, the structure of our bodies, nerves and brains being what it is, physical and*

mental torture (as well as disease and accident) can take such horrific forms."

What would Augustine and Irenaeus say to these ideas?

Does God's foreknowledge of the Fall of Man and subsequent evil make **GOD ULTIMATELY RESPONSIBLE** for it in Augustine's theodicy? Did God not have the power to make humans not able to sin, if he could see that we would? Augustine says:

> *"God indeed had the power to make humans who could not sin. But He preferred to make them so that they had the power to sin or not sin as they wished. As a result there would be humans who gained merit from not sinning in this life and who received in the next the reward of not being able to sin."*

Augustine seems to be saying that creating human beings able to sin is not the same as "they will sin", and having free will and the possible disastrous consequences of that is better than not having free will. But does this still make God responsible if he knew humanity would choose to use their free will for evil? Augustine responds by saying that humans are not compelled to sin by external factors, like a stone has no choice but to fall when dropped. **MORAL EVIL**, unlike the stone's fall, is a **VOLUNTARY** use of free will. Even though God's knowledge is perfect and must include knowledge of the fall of man, humans freely make choices. Augustine thinks God's omniscience and human freedom are compatible. Is this convincing?

KEY QUOTES

1. *"Either God cannot abolish evil, or He will not; if He cannot, then He is not all-powerful; if He will not, then He is not all-good."* Augustine

2. *"That which is the evil of all things in which any evil is perceptible is corruption. So the corruption of the educated mind is ignorance: the corruption of the just mind, injustice; the corruption of the brave mind, cowardice. In a living body the corruption of health is pain and disease."* Augustine

3. *"According to Augustine there was no evil in creation before angelic and human sin. It came into existence when first angels, and then humans misused their wills turning from their creator."* Saulytis

4. *"God must have been on leave during the Holocaust."* Wiesenthal

5. *"God judged it better to bring good out of evil than to suffer no evil to exist."* Augustine

6. *"The glory of God is the human person fully alive."* Irenaeus

7. *"A world which is to be a person-making environment cannot be a pain-free paradise but must contain challenges and dangers, with real possibilities of many kinds and disaster, and the pain and suffering which they bring."* Hick

8. *"In a world devoid both of dangers to be avoided and rewards to be won we may assume that there would have been virtually no moral development of the human intellect and imagination, and hence of either the sciences or the arts, and hence of human civilisation or culture."* Hick

9. *"Never shall I forget that night, the first night in camp, which has turned my life into one long night, seven times cursed and seven times sealed ... Never shall I forget those moments which murdered my God and my soul and turned my dreams to dust."* Elie Wiesel

10. *"Many have argued that there is a contradiction involved in the fact of evil and the belief in an omnipotent all-loving God. However, it does not seem logically contradictory, since it is not the same as saying, 'there is a God and there is no God'. It is not logically necessary that an omnipotent all-loving God prevents evil, and a theodicy is an attempt at a solution of the problem of evil, without denying God's omnipotence or love or the reality of evil. It shows God is justified in allowing evil."* Cole

CONFUSIONS TO AVOID

- Note that the theodicies are put forward to defend the existence of a God who has certain characteristics. To simply say that the existence of evil in the world means it is impossible to believe in God is not what this topic is about. **ARISTOTLE'S PRIME MOVER**-type God has nothing to do with the world and therefore the existence of suffering would not at all be an argument against such a God, as the Prime Mover is never once declared as loving or interested in humanity. Be careful to note that theodicies are trying to justify why a **POWERFUL AND LOVING GOD** allows evil.

- Highlight the differences between **AUGUSTINE** and **IRENAEUS**, as their theodicies differ in many ways. Be very clear that you are aware of their explanations of the source of natural and moral evil, the role of free will, the purpose of evil and the ongoing effect of evil in the world. If you do use Hick's development of Irenaeus, make sure you say that that is what you are doing.

GET MORE HELP

Get more help with the problem of evil by using the links below:

http://i-pu.sh/J2P31S46

Exam Rescue Remedy

1. Build your own scaffolding which represents the logic of the theory. Use a mind map or a summary sheet.

2. Do an analysis of past questions by theme as well as by year. Try writing your own Philosophy of Religion paper based on what hasn't come up recently.

3. Examine examiners' reports for clues as to how to answer a question well.

4. Use the **AREA** approach suggested in this revision guide. **ARGUMENT** - Have I explained the argument (from Plato or Kant for example)? **RESPONSE** - Have I outlined and explained a good range of responses to the argument? **EVALUATION** - Now I have clearly set out positions, what do I think of these? Is mine **A PHILOSOPHICAL** argument, and why? Does the original argument stand or fall against the criticisms raised? Why or why not?

5. List relevant technical vocabulary for inclusion in essay (eg efficient cause, form of the good, analytic, synthetic).

6. Prepare key quotes from selected key authors, original/ contemporary - even better, produce your own. Learn some.

7. Contrast and then evaluate different views/theories/authors as some questions ask "which approach is best?" So contrast every approach with one other and decide beforehand what you think.

8. Practise writing for 35 minutes. Don't use a computer, unless you will do so in the exam.

9. Always answer and discuss the exact question in front of you; never learn a "model answer". Use your own examples (newspapers, films, documentaries, real life). Be prepared to think creatively and adapt your knowledge to the question.

10. Conclude with your view, justify it (give reasons) especially with "discuss".

BIBLIOGRAPHY

- **AHLUWALIA, L** - Understanding Philosophy of Religion OCR, Folens, 2008

- **BARON, P** - Religious Studies (AS Ethics), PushMe Press, 2011

- **BOWIE, R** - AS/A2 Philosophy of Religion and Religious Ethics for OCR, Nelson Thornes, 2004

- **COLE, P** - Access to Philosophy: Philosophy of Religion, Hodder & Stoughton, 2005

- **DEWAR, G** - Oxford Revision Guides: AS & A Level Religious Studies: Philosophy and Ethics Through Diagrams, Oxford University Press, 2009

- **JACKSON, R** - The God of Philosophy, The Philosophers' Magazine, 2001

- **JORDAN, A, LOCKYER, N** & **TATE, E** - Philosophy of Religion for A Level OCR Edition, Nelson Thornes, 2004

- **LACEWING, M** - Philosophy for AS, Routledge, 2008

- **PHELAN, JW** - Philosophy Themes and Thinkers, Cambridge University Press, 2005

- **RICHARDS, HJ** - Philosophy of Religion, Heinemann, 2004

- **RUSSELL, B** - History of Western Philosophy, Routledge Classics, 1946 (2008).

- **TAYLOR, I, EYRE, C** & **KNIGHT, R** - OCR Religious Studies Philosophy and Ethics AS, Heinemann, 2008

- **TAYLOR, M** - OCR Philosophy of Religion for AS and A2, Routledge, 2009

- **THOMPSON, M** - An Introduction to Philosophy and Ethics, Hodder & Stoughton, 2009

- **WILKINSON, M** & **CAMPBELL, H** - Philosophy of Religion for AS Level, Continuum, 2009

Lightning Source UK Ltd.
Milton Keynes UK
UKOW03f1358270214

227285UK00002B/15/P